THE LITTLE BOOK OF

SNEAKERS

First published in Great Britain in 2026 by Cassell,
an imprint of
Octopus Publishing Group Ltd
Carmelite House
50 Victoria Embankment
London EC4Y 0DZ
www.octopusbooks.co.uk

An Hachette UK Company
www.hachette.co.uk

The authorized representative in the EEA is
Hachette Ireland
8 Castlecourt Centre, Dublin 15, D15 XTP3
email: info@hbgi.ie

Distributed in the US by Hachette Book Group
1290 Avenue of the Americas, 4th and 5th Floors
New York, NY 10104

Distributed in Canada by Canadian Manda Group
664 Annette St., Toronto, Ontario, Canada
M6S 2C8

This book was conceived, designed, and
produced by The Bright Press, an imprint of the
Quarto Group,
1 Triptych Place, 185 Park Street,
London, United Kingdom, SE1 9SH
T (0)2077 009 000
www.Quarto.com

Publisher: James Evans
Editorial Director: Isheeta Mustafi
Managing Editor: Lucy Tipton
Art Director: Emily Nazer
Commissioning Editor: Caroline Elliker
Project Editor: Katie Crous
Design and Picture Research: Anna Gatt

ISBN: 978-1-78840-697-0
eISBN: 978-1-78840-710-6

A CIP catalogue record for this book is available from the British Library.

Printed and bound in Guangdong, China.

TT/06/26

10 9 8 7 6 5 4 3 2 1

MIX
Paper | Supporting responsible forestry
FSC® C016973
FSC
www.fsc.org

This FSC® label means that materials used for the product have been responsibly sourced.

THE LITTLE BOOK OF SNEAKERS

THE ILLUSTRATED GUIDE TO ICONIC BRANDS AND CLASSIC DESIGNS

ALEX MILLS

CONTENTS

INTRODUCTION 6

ORIGINS AND EVOLUTION OF SNEAKER CULTURE 8

- From Athletics to Self-expression
- From Basketball to High Fashion
- Anatomy of a Sneaker
- Sneakerheads and Collecting
- Timeline

ICONIC SNEAKERS THAT CHANGED THE GAME 28

- Converse Chuck Taylor All Star
- Adidas Stan Smith
- Puma Suede
- Adidas Superstar
- Nike Cortez
- New Balance 990
- Nike Air Jordan 1
- Nike Air Force 1
- Nike Air Jordan 3
- Vans Old Skool
- Nike Dunk
- Reebok Classic
- Nike Air Max 1
- Adidas Gazelle
- ASICS GEL-Lyte III

LEGENDARY DESIGNERS AND COLLABORATIONS **78**

- Tinker Hatfield
- Virgil Abloh
- Kanye West
- Rei Kawakubo
- Hiroshi Fujiwara
- Nike x Supreme
- Air Jordan x Dior
- Adidas x Yohji Yamamoto

BRAND SPOTLIGHTS **106**

- Nike
- Adidas
- Puma
- New Balance
- Vans
- Converse
- Expanding Field

Index **140**
Picture credits **142**
Author Acknowledgements **143**
Raising Readers **144**

INTRODUCTION

Long before sneakers became objects of style and collecting, they were practical solutions to specific problems. Early sports shoes were designed with function in mind, offering grip, protection and support for athletes at a time when specialist footwear barely existed. Simple rubber soles and canvas uppers marked a clear break from formal leather shoes, creating something lighter, cheaper and better suited to movement.

BEYOND FUNCTIONALITY

As organized sport expanded through the twentieth century, so did the sneaker. Basketball, running and tennis each demanded different performance features, and brands responded with new materials, cushioning systems and manufacturing techniques. By the late twentieth century, sneakers were no longer confined to courts or tracks. They appeared on city streets, shaped by music scenes, youth movements and subcultures that adopted particular styles as markers of identity. This book traces that shift through the sneakers themselves, the brands and designers who created them, and the cultures the sneakers came to represent.

RIGHT: Crazy Legs of the Rock Steady Crew wearing Adidas sneakers, early hip hop culture, 1982.

32
CLEVELAND
BROWNS
49
CLEVELAND
BROWNS
CLEVELAND
BROWNS

ORIGINS AND EVOLUTION OF SNEAKER CULTURE

FROM ATHLETICS TO SELF-EXPRESSION

The earliest sneakers in the United States and Britain emerged in the late nineteenth and early twentieth centuries, following the development of vulcanized rubber. Early examples came from companies such as US Rubber (Keds), Converse and the Liverpool Rubber Company, later known as Dunlop. Rubber soles offered grip and flexibility, making them well suited to activities such as tennis, basketball and general training. Canvas uppers kept shoes lightweight and relatively affordable, helping standardize athletic footwear across growing sports communities.

At this stage, sneakers were specialist equipment. They were worn for sport and little else, valued for function rather than appearance. Design choices focused on durability and performance, with little variation between models.

PREVIOUS PAGES: American football players training outdoors, showing early use of specialist athletic footwear, 1959.
RIGHT: Early rubber-soled sneakers introduced grip and flexibility, shaping modern athletic footwear.

You feel like
Jumping for Joy
in U.S. Keds®
The Shoes of Champions
From the instant you step inside U. S. Keds, your foot feels springy as a lion's paw . . . and so light you might be barefoot! U. S. Keds cushion your heel, cushion your arch, cushion your toes. You can keep on going in U. S. Keds . . . hardly ever tire! No wonder man, woman and child, everybody "jumps for joy" in U. S. Keds—there's no substitute for 'em!
SHOCKPROOF ARCH CUSHION
HEEL-TO-TOE CUSHIONED INSOLE
CUSHIONED SHOCKPROOF HEEL
U.S. Keds
THIS BLUE KEDS LABEL STAMPS THE SHOE OF CHAMPIONS
BOOSTER
CHAMPION
CAGER
CHAMPION STRAP
US RUBBER
United States Rubber
ROCKEFELLER CENTER, NEW YORK 20, N. Y.
IN CANADA: DOMINION RUBBER COMPANY, LTD.

CLYDE
Walt "Clyde" Frazier
Clydes. The essence of cool.
Inspired by basketball legend Walt Frazier, these suedes let you play it cool, both on and off the court. And the choice of color combinations is virtually endless.
PUMA
PUMA
Our word for quality.

MOVING INTO EVERYDAY LIFE

Sneakers began to appear outside athletic settings through everyday use rather than deliberate cultural positioning. Athletes, including basketball players such as Chuck Taylor and, later, stars like Walt 'Clyde' Frazier, wore them off-duty, favouring their comfort and practicality. Their lightweight construction and flexible soles made them suitable for long hours on foot, particularly in urban environments.

This shift did not happen all at once. Sneakers were still largely seen as informal footwear, worn casually rather than intentionally. However, their growing presence in daily life marked an important change. Shoes designed for sport were no longer confined to it.

As sneakers became more common in everyday settings, choice began to matter. Colour, brand and silhouette started to signal preference and affiliation.

LEFT: Athlete Walt 'Clyde' Frazier featured in Puma's Clyde campaign linking basketball style to everyday wear.

IDENTITY AND SELF-EXPRESSION

Once sneakers had become identity markers in the 1970s and early 1980s, they carried social information. Wearing a particular pair could suggest where someone lived, how they spent their time or what they valued. For example, Adidas Superstars worn by hip hop fans in New York, Puma Suedes associated with breakdancing crews, and Vans adopted by skateboarders in California, allowing footwear to function as a subtle form of self-expression.

STREET STYLE

The 1980s and 1990s marked a turning point in sneaker visibility. Hip hop culture brought sneakers onto stages, album covers and television screens, placing them in front of global audiences. Shoes became part of performance and image through artists such as Run-D.M.C. and the Beastie Boys and TV shows such as *Yo! MTV Raps*.

Streetwear brands such as Stüssy, FUBU and Karl Kani developed alongside this shift, connecting clothing, music and footwear into a shared visual language. Sneakers were now central to how artists and fans presented themselves, accelerating their shift from everyday items into cultural symbols.

ABOVE: The Beastie Boys wearing Adidas high-top sneakers, helping bring sneakers into music and street culture.

FROM BASKETBALL TO HIGH FASHION

When Michael Jordan entered the NBA in 1984, Nike was a challenger brand in basketball, better known for running shoes than those for the basketball court. Established court brand leaders Converse and Adidas produced shoes that were worn by most NBA players at the time. The Air Jordan 1 (see page 52) emerged as part of Nike's effort to establish itself in professional basketball through its partnership with Jordan, and it could be said that from then on, basketball played a parallel role in expanding sneaker culture.

The sport's growing media presence and international reach brought players and their footwear into focus. Signature models tied shoes to individual athletes, increasing recognition and desire.

This visibility operated at scale. Basketball sneakers were seen regularly, worn in high-pressure moments and associated with performance, confidence and ambition. The link between sport, personality and footwear strengthened, helping sneakers reach audiences far beyond the court.

LEFT: Michael Jordan wearing Air Jordan I during an NBA game with the Chicago Bulls, around 1985.

GLOBAL CULTURE LOCALLY EXPRESSED

Sneaker culture took on local characteristics in different regions. In Europe, from the late 1970s through the 1980s and 1990s, football terrace culture influenced styles and silhouettes, with fans adopting models such as Adidas Samba, Gazelle and Spezial as everyday footwear. In Japan, attention to detail, limited releases and archival interest shape how sneakers are collected and discussed. New York remains closely tied to basketball, hip hop and street-level wear. Here, sneakers often function as daily essentials, shaped by practicality and visibility.

SNEAKERS ON SOCIAL MEDIA

How sneaker culture is shared and understood has been transformed by social media. Platforms such as Instagram and TikTok spread trends quickly, often without formal brand or retailer endorsement. Visibility now comes from repetition and reach, with shoes gaining recognition through daily posts.

Taste is now shaped by stylists, runners, skaters and everyday wearers. The emphasis of online sneaker content often falls on fit, comfort and versatility, reflecting how people actually live in their shoes.

RIGHT: Adidas Samba and Gazelle styles worn casually linked football terrace culture to everyday dress.

LUXURY AND HIGH FASHION

For much of the twentieth century, high fashion positioned itself in contrast to sportswear. That boundary began to soften in the late 1990s and early 2000s as designers acknowledged sneakers' cultural presence and everyday legitimacy. Paris in particular has acted as a meeting point between fashion and street culture, with sneakers moving between luxury and everyday contexts.

Design houses such as Prada, Balenciaga and Louis Vuitton brought sneakers onto the runway as well as into luxury boutiques, reworking athletic silhouettes with premium materials such as Italian leather, suede and technical mesh. Sneakers were presented alongside tailored clothing in fashion shows and editorial campaigns, reframing them as fashion objects. Prices reflected this shift, with designer sneakers often selling for several hundred dollars, far above typical sportswear releases.

This shift did not replace existing meanings but rather added new ones. Athletic footwear became acceptable and desirable within fashion systems that had previously excluded it.

LEFT: A runway model wearing Nike Air Max sneakers during the Huffer show, New Zealand Fashion Week, 2018.

ANATOMY OF A SNEAKER

Sneakers are built from layered components that balance comfort, durability and performance. Each element has a defined role, shaping how the shoe fits, feels and functions in everyday use.

1. *Pull tab*: Loop at the heel or tongue to help pull the shoe on
2. *Padded collar/top line:* Cushioned edge around the ankle for comfort and support
3. *Tongue:* Layer beneath the laces that protects the foot and distributes pressure
4. *Laces:* Fastening system used to secure the shoe
5. *Eyelet:* Reinforced holes through which laces pass
6. *Eyestay:* Panel that holds the eyelets and supports lace tension
7. *Toe box/vamp:* Front upper section covering the toes
8. *Inner tongue:* Internal lining of the tongue for comfort and structure
9. *Foxing/heel:* Rear structure that stabilizes the heel
10. *Midsole/heel seat:* Cushioned layer providing shock absorption and support
11. *Outsole:* Bottom surface that contacts the ground and provides traction
12. *Mud guard:* Protective overlay wrapping the lower upper, guarding against wear
13. *Quarter overlay:* Panel on the side of the shoe adding structure and support
14. *Insole:* Internal footbed providing cushioning and underfoot comfort

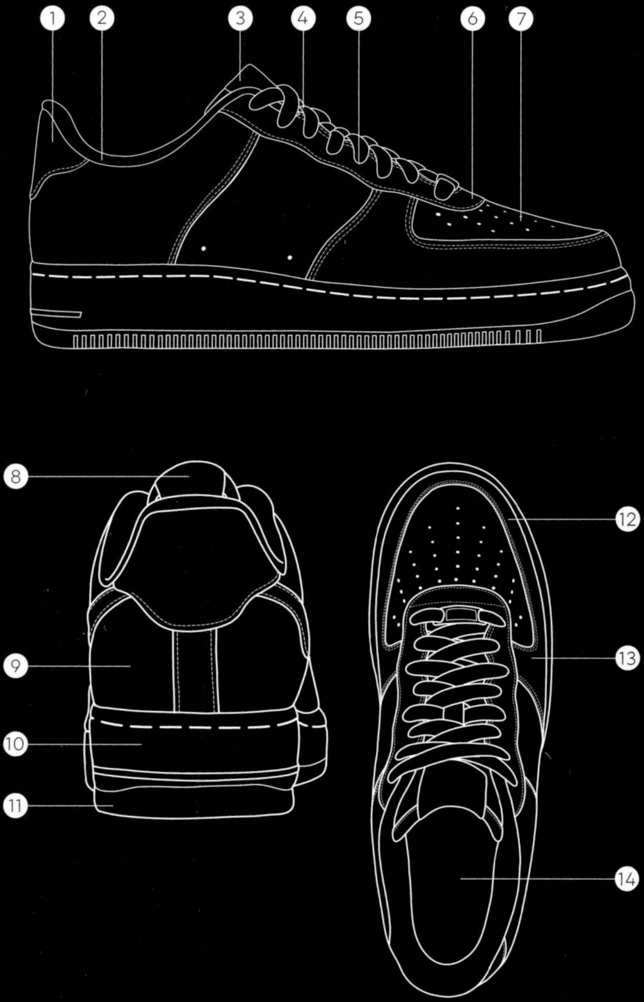
1
2
3
4
5
6
7
8
9
10
11
12
13
14

SNEAKERHEADS AND COLLECTING

In the 1980s, early sneaker collections often formed around basketball and hip hop in cities such as New York and Chicago. Fans searched for specific models worn by athletes or musicians, travelling between neighbourhood stores to find particular colourways.

During the 1990s and early 2000s, limited releases, brand collaborations and scheduled product drops created anticipation. Websites and early online forums allowed collectors to track releases, trade pairs and share information.

The rise of resale platforms and social media saw sneakers begin to circulate within a global secondary market, with certain releases gaining significant value. Instagram, YouTube and dedicated marketplaces helped collectors display their collections, discuss releases and influence demand. What had once been a niche hobby developed into a multibillion-dollar industry spanning fashion, media and investment.

Yet collecting remains personal. Some collectors focus on a single brand, silhouette or era; others build broader archives. For some, sneakers remain unworn and carefully stored; others wear theirs daily as part of their identity and style.

ABOVE: Sneaker collections organized by colour and model, showing the scale and intent behind modern collecting.

TIMELINE

1890s–1910s

Rubber-soled athletic shoes appear. Early brands include US Rubber (Keds), Converse and Dunlop.

1920s–1930s

Canvas basketball shoes become standardized. Converse All Star gains popularity in basketball.

1950s–1960s

Sneakers begin appearing in everyday youth culture, influenced by film, sport and casual dress.

1970s

Running boom drives innovation in cushioning and materials. Nike and Adidas expand globally.

1980s

Basketball and hip hop increase sneaker visibility. Key releases include the Air Jordan 1 (1985).

1990s

Collecting culture grows. Limited editions and collaborations become more common.

2000s

Luxury fashion begins embracing sneakers. Designers bring athletic silhouettes onto runways.

2010s

Social media accelerates sneaker trends. Resale platforms turn rare releases into investment pieces.

2020s

Greater focus on sustainability, recycled materials and new manufacturing technologies.

ICONIC SNEAKERS THAT CHANGED THE GAME

CONVERSE
ALL STAR

CONVERSE
ALL★STAR

CONVERSE
ALL★STAR

CONVERSE CHUCK TAYLOR ALL STAR

The Converse All Star began life as a basketball shoe in the early twentieth century, at a time when the sport itself was still finding its feet. First released in 1917, it was adopted widely by players for its lightweight construction and flexible rubber sole. In 1923, the shoe took on the name of Chuck Taylor, a semi-professional basketball player and Converse salesman who travelled the country promoting the shoe, running clinics and feeding back directly into its design.

Technically, the All Star was simple even by the standards of its time. A canvas upper, vulcanized rubber sole and minimal cushioning offered little in the way of performance innovation, but the shoe's straightforward construction made it durable, affordable and easy to produce at scale. For decades, it became the default basketball shoe in the United States, worn by players at every level.

AN UNASSUMING ICON

Its significance grew after basketball moved on. As the sport professionalized and footwear technology advanced, the All Star slipped out of elite competition and into everyday life. Musicians, artists and youth subcultures adopted it precisely because it was unassuming. By the late twentieth century, it had become a staple of punk, indie and skate scenes, valued for its neutrality and lack of branding excess.

Today, the Chuck Taylor All Star endures less as a sports shoe than as a cultural constant. Its form has barely changed, yet it continues to reappear across generations, styles and scenes, proving that longevity sometimes comes from restraint rather than reinvention.

SNEAKER FACTS

First release:	1917
Construction:	Canvas upper, vulcanized rubber sole
Design focus:	Lightweight, flexible, easy to manufacture
Why it matters:	Proved that a simple, unchanged design could stay relevant for generations.

adidas

stan smith
stan smith

ADIDAS STAN SMITH

Few sneakers have relied so heavily on subtlety. The Stan Smith has no visible stripes, no aggressive branding and little interest in novelty (although there have been some special editions), yet it has remained part of everyday dress for decades. Its appeal has never depended on moments of hype or reinvention, but on a design that never ages.

The shoe began life in the mid-1960s as a tennis model developed for French player Robert Haillet. When American tennis champion Stan Smith took over the endorsement in the late 1970s, his name replaced Haillet's, but the shoe itself changed very little. Built from smooth leather with perforated detailing at the sides, it was designed for durability, stability and long hours on court rather than visual impact.

A CLASSIC ALL-ROUNDER

That lack of emphasis proved decisive once the shoe drifted away from professional tennis. As performance footwear became more specialized, the Stan Smith moved quietly into everyday use, particularly across Europe. Its clean profile and neutral palette made it easy to wear, cutting across age, gender and subculture without being tied to any single scene.

Today, the Stan Smith functions as a benchmark for simplicity in sneaker design. It continues to appear in updated materials and colours, but its core appeal remains unchanged. In a category often driven by excess, its longevity comes from knowing when to stop.

SNEAKER FACTS

First release:	1965 (as the Haillet), renamed Stan Smith in the early 1970s
Construction:	Smooth leather upper, flat rubber sole
Design focus:	Minimal detailing, easy to wear with anything
Why it matters:	Became the world's go-to clean, white trainer, worn across styles and generations.

adidas
'STAN SMITH'
Endorsed by:

PUMA
SUEDE

PUMA
PUMA

PUMA SUEDE

The Puma Suede occupies a space between sport and style that few sneakers manage as naturally. First released in 1968, the Suede was developed as a low-profile athletic shoe at a time when basketball and training footwear were becoming lighter and more flexible. Its defining feature was the use of suede rather than smooth leather, giving the shoe a softer texture and a more relaxed appearance. A simple rubber sole and Puma's side Formstrip completed a design that prioritized balance and wearability over technical display.

CONSISTENT STRUCTURE

The shoe's cultural reach expanded rapidly. In the 1970s and 1980s, the Puma Suede became closely associated with breakdancing and hip hop, valued for its grip, durability and understated style. It also found a home on European football terraces and later within skate and casual street scenes, adapting easily to different contexts without losing its core shape.

Unlike sneakers that rely on reinvention, the Suede has endured through consistency. Updates have arrived through colour and material instead of structural change, allowing it to remain relevant without chasing trends. Today, it stands as a reminder that influence can be cumulative, built over decades of everyday wear rather than singular moments of attention.

SNEAKER FACTS

First release:	1968
Construction:	Suede upper, rubber sole
Design focus:	Low-profile shape, grip, everyday durability
Why it matters:	Became a defining shoe of early hip hop and street dance culture.

PUMA
SUEDE

SUPERSTAR
SUPERSTAR

adidas
adidas

ADIDAS SUPERSTAR

The Adidas Superstar is one of the clearest examples of a performance shoe reshaping everyday style without being designed to do so. Its journey from professional basketball courts to global streetwear staple was gradual, driven by visibility and adoption rather than deliberate reinvention.

Introduced in 1969, the Superstar was developed as a low-top basketball shoe at a time when leather uppers were still uncommon in the sport. Its most distinctive feature was the rubber shell toe, designed to protect players' feet during aggressive play. Combined with a supportive leather upper and durable sole, the shoe offered a level of protection and structure that appealed to elite athletes. By the early 1970s, it had been adopted by a large proportion of NBA players, firmly establishing its performance credentials.

INSTANTLY IDENTIFIABLE

The shoe's cultural reach expanded beyond basketball in the 1980s. As hip hop emerged as a visible force in popular culture, the Superstar became closely associated with artists and fans alike. Its clean shape, hard-wearing construction and recognizable silhouette suited both stage and street, and its presence in music and fashion helped move it into everyday wear. The relationship between Adidas and Run-D.M.C. formalized that shift, linking the shoe to a wider cultural identity.

What has kept the Superstar in circulation is not flexibility but recognizability. The shell toe, thick sole and compact proportions make it instantly identifiable, even when stripped of colour or context. While trends have moved towards slimmer or more technical silhouettes, the Superstar has remained deliberately solid. Its continued presence owes less to reinvention than to the way its shape has become embedded in collective memory, functioning as a fixed point within a constantly shifting sneaker landscape.

SNEAKER FACTS

First release:	1969
Construction:	Leather upper, rubber shell toe
Design focus:	Protection, durability, court-ready structure
Why it matters:	Helped take hip hop style from the streets to the global mainstream.

NIKE
NIKE

NIKE CORTEZ

The Nike Cortez was developed as a long-distance running shoe at a time when the sport was gaining wider visibility. Released in 1972, it focused on comfort and durability, offering cushioning designed to handle repeated miles instead of short bursts of speed. In an era when performance footwear was still relatively unspecialized, the Cortez addressed the needs of everyday runners, and not so much elite competition.

Designed by Bill Bowerman during Nike's earliest years, the shoe evolved from the Onitsuka Tiger Corsair, a model Bowerman had previously developed while working with the Japanese brand. After Nike separated from Onitsuka Tiger in the early 1970s, the design was reworked and released as the Nike Cortez. Its construction was straightforward and practical. A cushioned foam midsole reduced impact, while a grippy rubber outsole provided stability on the road. The low-profile shape and simple upper made it widely accessible, helping it reach a broad audience beyond sport.

A COMMUNITY CONSTANT

The Cortez's wider significance emerged as it moved into daily life. By the late 1970s and 1980s, it had become a familiar sight in everyday settings, particularly on the US West Coast. Comfortable, affordable and easy to wear, it was adopted by Chicano and Latino communities in Los Angeles, where it became part of a visual language tied to place, routine and continuity rather than trend.

Film and television reinforced that role. Appearances in popular culture presented the Cortez as a lived-in, everyday shoe, helping fix it in the public imagination. Nike later reflected this broader audience through variations such as the Señorita Cortez, adapting proportions while keeping the original form intact.

SNEAKER FACTS

First release:	1972
Construction:	Nylon or leather upper, cushioned foam midsole
Design focus:	Comfort and durability for long-distance running
Why it matters:	Became a symbol of everyday life on the US West Coast, reinforced by its appearance in the 1994 film *Forrest Gump*.

ENCAP
990
ENCAP
990

NEW BALANCE 990

The New Balance 990 was introduced in 1982 as a high-end running shoe, designed to bring stability, cushioning and flexibility together in a single model. It was positioned as a serious product for runners who valued function and build quality. Manufactured in the United States, the 990 set the template for what would become New Balance's 99X series. Its layered construction, supportive midsole and muted colour palette balanced technical detail with visual restraint.

The 990 found an audience in everyday settings, particularly in East Coast cities where comfort and reliability mattered. Unlike many heritage models, it has continued to change. New versions introduced updated cushioning systems, revised fits and modern materials, keeping pace with contemporary expectations while remaining recognizable.

SNEAKER FACTS

First release:	1982
Construction:	Layered upper with cushioned midsole, made in the USA
Design focus:	Stability, comfort and durability for daily running
Why it matters:	One of the first running shoes sold as a premium product.

NIKE AIR JORDAN 1

Designed by Peter Moore and released in 1985, the Air Jordan 1 was built for professional basketball but arrived with a visual confidence that set it apart from what players were wearing at the time. The shoe's high cut offered ankle support while its leather upper and bold colour blocking stood out. Jordan wore the black and red version early in his rookie season, drawing attention for breaking NBA's guidelines. Whether formally banned or simply discouraged, the contrast between league conservatism and Jordan's presence on court became part of the shoe's early reputation.

Jordan's performances ensured the shoe was seen regularly, and its design became associated with a player whose profile was growing beyond basketball. The Air Jordan 1 also began to circulate off the court, picked up by fans who responded to its image and identity alongside its performance.

SNEAKER FACTS

First release:	1985
Construction:	Leather upper, rubber sole
Design focus:	Ankle support, durability, bold colour blocking
Why it matters:	Showed how a basketball shoe could become a platform for an athlete's identity.

AIR

AIR

NIKE AIR FORCE 1

When the Air Force 1 was released in 1982, it represented a technical step forward for basketball footwear. Designed by Bruce Kilgore, a Nike footwear designer working on performance basketball shoes at the time, it was the first Nike model to feature a full-length Air cushioning unit. The high-cut silhouette, padded collar and ankle strap were practical responses to a faster, more physical game rather than stylistic flourishes.

On court, the shoe performed as intended, but its wider significance emerged away from professional basketball. As newer performance models replaced it, the Air Force 1 began to circulate in everyday settings, particularly in urban centres. Its solid construction, clean panels and generous proportions made it adaptable, easy to wear and visually confident without depending on novelty.

A MARKER OF IDENTITY

By the late 1980s and 1990s, the Air Force 1 had become closely associated with hip hop and street culture, especially in New York. Regional colourways, limited runs and local releases gave the shoe a sense of place, turning it into a marker of identity rather than performance. White-on-white and black-on-black versions became staples, worn regularly as opposed to being preserved.

SNEAKER FACTS

First release:	1982
Construction:	Leather upper, cupsole, Nike Air cushioning
Design focus:	Basketball support and impact protection
Why it matters:	First Nike Air basketball shoe, later the 'uptown' uniform of New York streets.

AIR

NIKE AIR JORDAN 3

By the time the Air Jordan 3 was released in 1988, Michael Jordan's relationship with Nike was under strain. Two signature models had already appeared but neither had fully resolved the tension between performance, personality and presentation. The third would do all three at once.

Designed by Tinker Hatfield, a Nike architect turned footwear designer, the Air Jordan 3 marked a clear shift in how Jordan sneakers were conceived. The silhouette was lighter and more agile than its predecessors, responding directly to Jordan's movement on court. Visible Nike Air cushioning appeared for the first time on a Jordan model, bringing performance technology into view.

Equally important was what the shoe chose to emphasize. The Air Jordan 3 introduced the Jumpman logo, removing the Nike Swoosh entirely. This was a quiet but decisive change, signalling the emergence of Jordan as a brand in his own right. The use of elephant-print panels – textured overlays on the toe and heel inspired by elephant skin – added identity without overwhelming the design, giving the shoe a visual signature that felt considered.

A LASTING ALIGNMENT

The Jordan 3's impact extended beyond design. Its release coincided with one of the most celebrated periods of Jordan's career, including the 1988 NBA Slam Dunk Contest, where the shoe was worn on court and broadcast worldwide. Performance, image and storytelling aligned.

Where earlier Jordans announced themselves loudly, the Air Jordan 3 refined the message. It established a language that future models would build upon, shaping the Jordan line into something sustainable, recognizable and enduring.

SNEAKER FACTS

First release:	1988
Construction:	Leather upper with elephant-print panels and visible Air cushioning
Design focus:	Lighter, more agile basketball shoe with exposed performance tech
Why it matters:	First Jordan shoe to show Nike Air and clearly separate the line from Nike basketball.

JORDAN

VANS "OFF THE WALL"

VANS OLD SKOOL

Released in 1977, and known originally as the Vans Style 36, the Old Skool was developed in response to skaters needing something tougher than the early Vans. The Old Skool introduced leather panelling to reinforce high-wear areas, while retaining the vulcanized rubber sole that gave Vans its distinctive board feel.

The shoe was the first to feature Vans' now-familiar side stripe, sketched informally by co-founder Paul Van Doren as a structural addition to reinforce the upper.

The Old Skool's low profile, durable construction and straightforward design made it easy to wear outside the skate park. Punk musicians, artists and later hip hop artists took to it for these reasons. It was functional, affordable and visually neutral, allowing it to move between scenes.

SNEAKER FACTS

First release:	1977
Construction:	Canvas and suede upper, vulcanized rubber sole
Design focus:	Reinforced durability
Why it matters:	First Vans shoe designed specifically for skateboarding.

NIKE DUNK

The Nike Dunk was introduced in 1985 as a basketball shoe designed to meet a practical problem. College teams needed footwear that could match their colours, and Nike wanted a model that could be produced quickly, consistently and at scale. The Dunk answered that brief. Built on familiar tooling and released in a wide range of team colourways, it prioritized uniformity and availability over innovation.

On court, the shoe performed reliably, but its broader significance emerged through circulation rather than competition. As basketball footwear evolved, the Dunk remained in production, quietly moving into everyday use. Its simple panels, sturdy construction and low-profile shape made it adaptable, and the explosion of colourways gave it a visual flexibility that few models could match. Owning a pair often had less to do with performance than affiliation, whether to a team, a place or a palette.

FORGING NEW IDENTITIES

That flexibility proved crucial decades later. In the early 2000s, the Dunk was adopted by skateboarding communities, valued for its padded tongue, supportive build and durability. Nike's subsequent collaborations and limited releases expanded the shoe's reach without altering its underlying form.

NIKE
NIKE

NIKE

The Dunk's longevity comes from repetition. Released, re-released and worn across different settings, it has remained visible through familiarity rather than novelty. Its meaning has been shaped by use, making it one of the clearest examples of how a straightforward design can absorb new identities over time.

SNEAKER FACTS

First release:	1985
Construction:	Leather upper, rubber cupsole
Design focus:	Scalable basketball shoe built for multiple colourways
Why it matters:	Showed how colour and repetition could drive sneaker culture.

REEBOK CLASSIC

The Reebok Classic was introduced in 1983 as a running shoe, designed at a moment when athletic footwear was becoming lighter, cleaner and more streamlined. Built from soft leather with a low profile and minimal detailing, it favoured comfort and wearability over visible performance technology. The result was a shoe that felt immediately approachable.

While its sporting roots were clear, the Classic quickly found a wider audience. Its neutral shape and understated branding made it easy to wear beyond training, particularly as running footwear moved away from tracks and into everyday life. Unlike shoes tied closely to a single sport or scene, the Classic circulated broadly, worn for practicality as much as style.

RELIABLE FORM

Over time, that openness became its defining feature. The shoe appeared in a wide range of colourways, though white, black and red versions remained dominant. Variations followed, including slip-ons, high-top editions and collaborations, but the underlying form stayed consistent. The Classic rarely demanded attention and did not rely on scarcity to maintain interest.

Reebok

Reebok

Reebok
Reebok

Its cultural associations developed gradually. In the UK, the Reebok Classic became linked with street style and club culture in the late 1980s and 1990s, valued for its clean lines and versatility. Elsewhere, it functioned as a dependable everyday option. The shoe's endurance lies in its adaptability.

SNEAKER FACTS

First release:	1983
Construction:	Soft leather upper, EVA midsole, rubber outsole
Design focus:	Comfort, simplicity and everyday wearability
Why it matters:	One of the first designs to make sneakers socially acceptable without an associated sport or subculture.

NIKE AIR MAX 1

Nike's Air technology had existed for years, but the Air Max 1 (1987) made it visible for the first time. What had been hidden inside the midsole became the defining feature.

The idea came from designer Tinker Hatfield: by cutting away the heel, the shoe revealed its inner workings, shifting attention to structure. Early reactions were cautious, yet the cushioning proved durable in use and effective underfoot.

The Air Max's bold heel unit gave it a presence that translated well to the street, especially as colourways expanded and materials shifted. Later versions refined the silhouette, including the Air Max 90 (1990), which amplified the visible Air unit and became one of the most recognizable models in the line. Reissues have kept the Air Max in circulation, each release reinforcing the original idea.

SNEAKER FACTS

First release:	1987
Construction:	Mesh and synthetic upper, visible Air cushioning
Design focus:	Making performance technology visible
Why it matters:	Changed how sneaker technology was seen by putting it on display.

GAZELLE
adidas

GAZELLE

ADIDAS GAZELLE

The Adidas Gazelle first appeared in the mid-1960s as a lightweight training shoe, designed for versatility. Its low profile, flat sole and suede upper made it suitable for indoor training and general athletic use.

What set the Gazelle apart was clarity of form. The shoe stripped back excess structure in favour of balance and feel. As more technical models took over competitive sport, the Gazelle remained in circulation through everyday wear.

Perhaps due to its adaptability, the Gazelle became associated with football terraces across Europe, where its understated design suited the casual dress codes of match-day culture. From there, it was absorbed into music and youth scenes, particularly in the UK, where it appeared in club culture, Britpop and later revival movements. Each context added meaning without altering the shoe's core design.

SNEAKER FACTS

First release:	1966
Construction:	Suede upper, rubber sole
Design focus:	Lightweight training shoe with a low-profile silhouette
Why it matters:	Adopted by multiple generations and scenes without being redesigned.

GEL LYTE III
GEL LYTE III
asics

GEL LYTE III
asics

ASICS GEL-LYTE III

Released in 1990, the GEL-Lyte III marked a decisive shift in how performance running shoes could look and feel. Designed by Shigeyuki Mitsui, the model introduced a now-famous split tongue, a functional yet defining solution to improve fit and reduce pressure across the top of the foot. The lightweight materials used, the cushioned midsole and ASICS' GEL technology reflected the brand's focus on biomechanics, comfort and technical credibility.

As running silhouettes filtered into streetwear during the 2000s, the GEL-Lyte III found an audience beyond sport. Partnerships with boutiques and designers helped reposition the model without altering its core structure. Today, the GEL-Lyte III is valued for its clarity of purpose. It represents a moment when performance thinking produced an enduring form, and when innovation was driven by use rather than attention.

SNEAKER FACTS

First release:	1990
Construction:	Mesh and suede upper, split tongue, GEL cushioning
Design focus:	Improving comfort through design
Why it matters:	Introduced a split tongue that changed how running shoes fit and feel.

Y-3
Y-3
Y-3
YOHJI YAMAMOTO

LEGENDARY DESIGNERS AND COLLABORATIONS

TINKER HATFIELD

Occupying a distinctive position in sneaker history, Tinker Hatfield's influence runs through the design process as much as the product. Trained as an architect, he also happened to be an accomplished athlete at high school and university, coming sixth in pole vault in the 1976 Olympic trials. When he turned his talents to sneaker design, Hatfield brought a way of thinking about structure, proportion and visibility into a field that was becoming increasingly technical but was still visually conservative.

When Hatfield joined Nike in the early 1980s, performance innovation was advancing quickly, particularly around cushioning and materials. His work on the Air Max 1 changed how that progress was presented. By exposing the Air unit, the shoe made its construction readable. Wearers could see how it worked, and that visibility altered expectations around what a performance shoe could look like. Technology became part of the conversation, rather than something assumed.

PREVIOUS PAGES: Yohji Yamamoto's Y-3 combined sportswear construction with high fashion styling.
RIGHT: The Air Jordan 3 introduced visible Air cushioning and the Jumpman logo.

JOURNEY
BULLS
23
THE CHAMPION

CONFIDENCE WITHOUT EXCESS

That approach carried into basketball. Hatfield's designs for the Air Jordan line responded closely to how Michael Jordan moved on court, resulting in lighter silhouettes with clearer lines and a strong sense of balance. Details such as visible Air and distinctive panelling helped make the shoes immediately recognizable while remaining grounded in performance needs. The shoes communicated confidence without excess.

Inside Nike, Hatfield's impact extended beyond individual releases. He demonstrated that designers could influence storytelling through form and structure, helping to establish design as a central voice within the company. This shift created space for future experimentation and a more open relationship between innovation, narrative and product. His work spanned defining models including the Air Max 1, Air Trainer 1 and multiple Air Jordan silhouettes, as well as concept-driven projects such as the self-lacing Nike Air Mag, linking performance design with broader cultural storytelling.

TOP LEFT: The Nike Air Trainer 1, an early cross-training model designed by Tinker Hatfield.
LEFT: Hatfield with the Air Jordan XI, a key performance and design milestone in the Jordan line.

VIRGIL ABLOH

Virgil Abloh approached sneakers as a system of references. Trained in architecture and operating across fashion, music and design, he was less interested in perfecting form than in examining what objects meant, how they were read, and who felt invited into the conversation around them. Through his label Off-White, he applied the same approach to fashion, using quotation marks, industrial details and reworked staples to question how products are read.

His work with Nike, most visibly through 'The Ten' project, took familiar silhouettes and treated them as source material. Cuts, labels and exposed construction details drew attention to process, asking wearers to notice how shoes were assembled and classified. The designs did not disguise their origins. Instead, they made those origins part of the point. This approach encouraged a different kind of engagement, where understanding and recognition mattered as much as ownership.

Specific releases helped define the impact. The Air Jordan 1, Air Presto and Air Force 1, all from The Ten, became widely circulated and reinterpreted across both fashion and resale markets.

RIGHT: Off-White x Nike Air VaporMax featuring exposed stitching and visible Air cushioning.

"AIR"
NIKE
SHOELACES

A CLEAR LANGUAGE

Abloh's impact came from clarity of language. Quotation marks, zip ties and printed text functioned as cues, giving audiences a way to read design intention without specialist knowledge. Sneakers became annotated objects, carrying their own explanations. That accessibility helped broaden who felt comfortable participating in sneaker culture, especially younger audiences encountering these references for the first time.

Within Nike, Abloh's collaborations shifted expectations around authorship. His work suggested that a designer could operate as a visible presence rather than as an invisible hand, shaping conversation as well as product. The success of The Ten confirmed that experimentation and transparency could exist within a global brand framework.

Abloh's influence continues to be felt in how sneakers are discussed and presented. His work established a shared visual vocabulary that prioritized ideas, references and dialogue, leaving behind a model where meaning is built through context as much as through form.

TOP: Off-White x Air Jordan 1 from 'The Ten' collection, in deconstructed Chicago colourway.
BOTTOM LEFT: Virgil Abloh at an Off-White x Nike signing during Paris Fashion Week, 2017.
BOTTOM RIGHT: Off-White x Nike Zoom Fly SP featuring translucent upper and printed "FOAM" midsole text.

"SHOELACES"
"AIR"

NIKE

"FOAM"

KANYE WEST

Kanye West's impression on sneaker culture came from balancing the power in the relationship between creator and brand. When Yeezy launched with Adidas in the mid-2010s, it was built as a standalone product line, supported by dedicated design, development and distribution infrastructure.

Before Adidas, West had already entered sneaker design through Nike, releasing the Air Yeezy in 2009 and a follow-up in 2012. These projects were developed in collaboration with designers including Mark Smith and later influenced West's approach to building a more independent product line.

The shoes themselves reflected this ambition. Models such as the Yeezy Boost 350 and 700 moved away from traditional basketball or running silhouettes, favouring sculptural forms, muted colour palettes and an emphasis on comfort. Boost cushioning provided the technical foundation, but the visual identity was set by shape and texture more than performance cues. The result was footwear that felt distinct from existing Adidas categories while remaining recognizably part of the brand.

RIGHT: Adidas Yeezy Boost 350 'Zebra' featuring Primeknit upper and Boost sole unit.

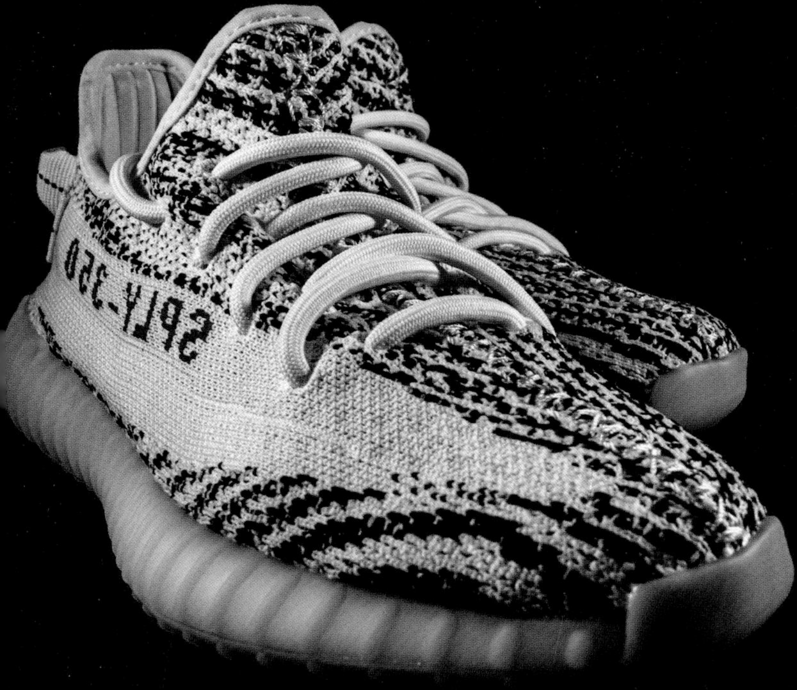
SPLY-350

SPLY-350

While West acted as the creative lead and public face of the line, the work was developed in collaboration with Adidas designers, including Steven Smith, whose experience in performance footwear helped translate those ideas into production.

FAR-REACHING

What set Yeezy apart was reach. Releases were scarce but not marginal. Demand operated at a global level, supported by coordinated launches, controlled supply and sustained attention across fashion and music media. Sneakers became events, and ownership became a signal of participation in a wider cultural moment rather than affiliation with a specific sport or scene.

The partnership showed that a single creative figure could influence product direction, marketing and consumer behaviour at scale. Even after the collaboration ended, its impact remained visible in how companies approached creator-led footwear lines. Yeezy's legacy helped to establish a model where cultural influence could be translated directly into industrial production, altering how sneakers are conceived, launched and valued.

TOP LEFT: Adidas Yeezy Boost 700 with sculpted sole unit and layered upper construction.
LEFT: Adidas Yeezy Boost 350 with Primeknit upper and responsive cushioning.

REI KAWAKUBO

Rei Kawakubo's impact on the sneaker industry comes from her ability to place familiar objects into unfamiliar contexts. As the founder of Comme des Garçons, she built a reputation for challenging established ideas of shape, proportion and finish in fashion. When sneakers entered that environment, they were handled with the same intent.

Collaborations between Comme des Garçons and sportswear brands brought well-known silhouettes into the fashion calendar. Shoes that were originally designed for courts or tracks appeared on runways and in concept-driven collections, often altered through material choice, surface treatment or scale. Logos were muted, colours restrained and proportions adjusted. The designs remained recognizable, but their setting changed how they were understood.

LEGITIMATELY FASHIONABLE

This shift mattered because it changed where sneakers were taken seriously. Seeing them presented alongside experimental clothing reframed them as legitimate fashion objects rather than casual additions.

RIGHT: Comme des Garçons x Converse Chuck Taylor collaboration with signature heart logo.

CONVERSE
PLAY

The shoes were no longer judged only by performance or heritage, but by how they sat within a broader visual language.

Kawakubo's work also influenced how collaboration itself was approached. The projects retained a clear sense of authorship, with Comme des Garçons' perspective remaining visible. This can be seen in collaborations with Nike on the Air Force 1 and Dunk, and with Converse on the Chuck Taylor, where familiar silhouettes were reworked through Comme des Garçons' lens using pared-back colour, altered proportions and unexpected material treatments. That clarity allowed sneakers to carry a fashion viewpoint without losing their original identity.

Kawakubo's contribution to sneaker culture lies in expanding where sneakers belong. By placing them within fashion's most experimental spaces, Kawakubo helped open the category to new interpretations that continue to shape how designers and brands approach footwear today.

TOP RIGHT: Comme des Garçons x Converse Chuck Taylor high-top with printed heart motif.
BOTTOM RIGHT: Comme des Garçons x Nike sneakers using layered construction and exaggerated proportions.

HIROSHI FUJIWARA

Hiroshi Fujiwara's influence on sneaker culture comes from his role as a connector. Based in Tokyo, he moved easily between music, streetwear and design at a time when those worlds were still relatively separate. Rather than focusing on a single silhouette or brand, Fujiwara helped shape how collaboration itself worked.

His relationship with Nike is central to that story. In the early 2000s, Fujiwara became part of the HTM project alongside, and named after, Tinker Hatfield and Nike CEO Mark Parker. It introduced a new way of developing products within a large sportswear company, bringing together design leadership, cultural insight and technical development in a small, focused unit. The shoes produced were understated and limited, but the process behind them proved influential.

Specific projects made that influence visible. Fujiwara's Fragment Design collaborations with Nike, including the Air Jordan 1, Air Force 1 and HTM Air Max releases, established a recognizable approach built on minimal colour palettes, subtle branding and small production runs.

ABOVE: Fragment Design x Nike Dunk High with minimal colour blocking and lightning bolt branding.

The Classic / Fragment : sacai

SIGNATURE RESTRAINT

Through Fragment Design (Fujiwara's Tokyo-based creative and design agency), Fujiwara applied a similar approach across multiple partnerships. His sneaker collaborations were typically restrained in colour and detailing, often using familiar models with minimal changes. Small cues such as lightning-bolt logos or subtle material shifts signalled authorship without overwhelming the original design. This restraint became part of his signature.

More importantly, Fujiwara helped normalize collaboration as an ongoing relationship rather than a one-off event. His projects were built on trust and continuity, establishing a framework that many brands later adopted. Limited runs, clear authorship and long-term partnerships became standard practice across the industry.

Fujiwara's impact is visible in how sneaker collaborations are structured today. By showing that cultural knowledge could guide product development without dominating it, he helped set the blueprint for modern sneaker partnerships that balance credibility, consistency and scale.

LEFT: Fragment Design x Air Jordan I and Nike Dunk collaborations with restrained palette and branding.

NIKE x SUPREME

The partnership between Nike and New York clothing brand Supreme helped define how modern sneaker collaboration works. Supreme had built credibility within skate culture through consistency and taste-making, while Nike brought scale, archive depth and production power. When the two came together in the early 2000s, the partnership felt natural to the audiences already invested in both.

Supreme's role was not to redesign Nike's shoes from scratch, but to focus attention on models that already carried meaning. Dunk, Air Force 1 and Air Max silhouettes were presented through limited releases, tight distribution and restrained branding. Small details, such as box logos or colour blocking, signalled involvement without overwhelming the original design.

Over time, the collaboration established a rhythm that became influential across the industry. Releases were spaced, demand was managed, and each drop felt connected to what came before. Nike × Supreme helped define how streetwear partnerships could operate inside a global brand, balancing credibility with scale and turning collaboration into a sustained relationship.

ABOVE: Supreme x Nike Air Force 1 collaboration released through a limited distribution strategy.

AIR JORDAN x DIOR

Marking a shift in how luxury fashion engaged with sneakers, when the Air Jordan 1 was selected for the collaboration in 2020, it was treated as a historical object with cultural weight, and not just a novelty adapted for the runway.

The design stayed close to the original silhouette, with changes concentrated in material quality and construction. Italian leather, refined finishing and subtle Dior branding elevated the shoe without altering its proportions. The familiarity of the form played a central role in its impact, allowing both sneaker and fashion audiences to recognize what they were looking at immediately.

What made the collaboration significant was its reframing of value. The shoe sat comfortably within luxury pricing and presentation, while remaining legible as an Air Jordan. It demonstrated that sneakers did not need to be transformed to be taken seriously in high fashion. Instead, their existing cultural authority could be acknowledged and built upon, setting a precedent for future luxury collaborations.

RIGHT: Air Jordan I x Dior collaboration using premium leather and co-branded detailing.

AIR DIOR

ADIDAS x YOHJI YAMAMOTO

Launched in the early 2000s under the Y-3 label, the collaboration between Adidas and Japanese fashion designer Yohji Yamamoto was conceived as a long-term project. It aimed to bring fashion-led thinking into Adidas' performance and development.

Yamamoto's influence reshaped how Adidas silhouettes were approached. Shoes produced under Y-3 emphasized proportion, material choice and silhouette, often using monochrome palettes and sculptural forms. Performance knowledge remained present, but it was expressed through design language rather than overt technical signalling.

Over time, Y-3 established its own audience and identity, separate from both Adidas' core performance lines and the fashion calendar. Its success showed that collaboration could function as a parallel design space built on continuity and trust. Adidas × Yohji Yamamoto helped define a model where sport and fashion could coexist long-term, influencing how brands structure creative partnerships today.

RIGHT: Y-3 footwear combining Adidas performance tooling with Yohji Yamamoto's design language.

Y-3
Y-3

CONVERSE
CONVERSE
CONVERSE

BRAND SPOTLIGHTS

NIKE

Nike was built on a simple premise: performance can always be improved. Founded in Oregon in the early 1970s by Phil Knight (a successful track runner and accountant) and coach Bill Bowerman, the company grew out of a close relationship between athletes, experimentation and problem-solving. Bowerman's approach to footwear design was practical and obsessive, focused on marginal gains. That mindset has remained central to Nike's identity, even as the brand scaled globally. Nike does not position itself as a heritage label. Instead, it frames itself as a continual work in progress, where innovation, testing and iteration are treated as core values and not just marketing claims.

SIGNATURE MODELS

Few brands have produced as many defining silhouettes across different sports and eras. From early running shoes like the Cortez, to basketball models such as the Air Jordan line and the Air Force 1, Nike's most enduring designs tend to share a common trait: they solved a specific problem before

TOP RIGHT: Bill Bowerman, Nike co-founder, known for early experimentation in running shoe design.
BOTTOM: Bowerman with Oregon athletes, reflecting his performance-led development process.

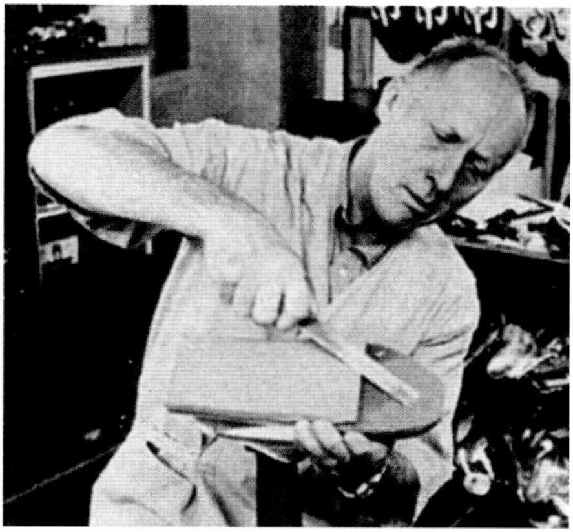

NCAA
UNIVERSITY
EGON
LAP
FIRST DOWNS
OREGON
20

becoming cultural objects. Even models that later took on symbolic meaning often began life as highly functional tools. This grounding in performance helps explain why so many Nike shoes transition easily into everyday wear. They arrive with a built-in credibility that does not rely on fashion cycles alone.

INNOVATION STORIES

Nike's influence has often come from its willingness to expose technology. The visible Air unit, first introduced in the late 1980s, turned cushioning into a design feature and shifted how consumers understood performance footwear. More recently, lightweight knitted uppers, carbon-fibre plates in running shoes and data-led design processes have reinforced Nike's role as a technical leader. Crucially, innovation at Nike is rarely isolated to a single product. New materials and systems tend to filter across categories, shaping the broader lineup rather than existing as one-off statements.

LEFT: The Air Jordan I achieved a cultural status beyond its basketball origins.

SCALE, CULTURE AND CONTROL

Nike's size allows it to operate at multiple speeds. It can support elite athletes, develop specialist performance products and still influence mass-market style. That reach has also shaped the modern resale economy, where scarcity, storytelling and controlled releases play a growing role. Yet Nike's dominance has never depended on exclusivity alone. Its most successful moments usually combine wide visibility with a clear point of view, ensuring the brand remains both aspirational and familiar. In doing so, Nike has become less a single label than an infrastructure, setting the pace for how the sneaker industry operates as a whole.

Nike's reach is reinforced through athletes such as Michael Jordan (Air Jordan), Serena Williams, Cristiano Ronaldo and LeBron James, whose signature lines and on-court visibility have driven both performance innovation and global demand.

RIGHT: Partnerships across sports expanded Nike's influence on athletic performance and culture, from tennis (Serena Williams, top left) through basketball (LeBron James, top right) to football (Cristiano Ronaldo, bottom).

ALL-STAR

ADIDAS

Shaped by origin in a way few sportswear brands are, Adidas was founded in Germany in the early twentieth century by Adi Dassler, a trained shoemaker who began making athletic footwear in his mother's laundry. The company grew out of a belief that athletes deserved equipment designed precisely for their sport. Following a fractured personal and business relationship between the Dassler brothers, Adi's brother Rudolf went on to establish Puma, creating a second major sportswear brand from the same roots. Adidas, however, defined itself through scale, consistency and institutional trust instead of rivalry. Precision, fit and sport-specific purpose have remained central to the brand's identity, even as it expanded globally, with authority built through repetition and credibility.

SIGNATURE MODELS

Adidas' most recognizable sneakers often began life far from fashion. Shoes such as the Superstar, Stan Smith, Gazelle and Samba were created for basketball, tennis, training and football, respectively,

TOP: Adi Dassler, founder of Adidas.
BOTTOM LEFT: Dassler working in early shoe production.
BOTTOM RIGHT: Chelsea FC defender Ron Harris prepares for play in Adidas football boots, designed for traction and control.

each shaped by the demands of its original sport. Their later adoption into everyday dress came through repetition as opposed to reinvention. These models appeared on courts, terraces and streets for decades, building familiarity across generations. As a result, Adidas classics tend to feel embedded rather than reintroduced. They function as reference points within culture, returning in new contexts without losing their original character.

INNOVATION STORIES

While Adidas is often associated with heritage, its technical contributions are substantial. The brand has consistently explored cushioning systems, lightweight construction and performance materials, from early studded football boots to modern running technologies. In more recent years, Adidas has balanced this legacy with experimentation, particularly through its Boost cushioning platform and advances in knit uppers. Innovation at Adidas often arrives quietly, integrated into established silhouettes instead of being presented as radical departures. This approach reinforces trust among athletes and consumers alike, positioning progress as an extension of expertise rather than a reset.

LEFT: Model Bella Hadid wearing Adidas SL 72 sneakers, highlighting the revival of archival silhouettes.

CULTURE AND COLLABORATION

Adidas' cultural impact has been shaped by long-term relationships more than rapid turnover. Its visibility within football culture, hip hop and later streetwear developed through sustained presence, from European terraces to New York stages. Partnerships with artists and designers have expanded its reach, with key collaborations including Run-D.M.C.'s endorsement of the Superstar in the 1980s, Yohji Yamamoto's Y-3 line, Pharrell Williams' Hu series, Kanye West's Yeezy line, before his departure, and long-running projects with Stella McCartney and Raf Simons.

Still, the brand's identity remains anchored by its archive. Unlike brands that constantly reinvent their image, Adidas tends to circle back to familiar forms, allowing context to change around them. That continuity has made Adidas less reactive to trends and more resilient to shifts in taste, securing its place as a constant within an industry defined by change.

TOP: Run-D.M.C. helped establish the Adidas Superstar as a defining sneaker within hip hop culture.
BOTTOM: Adidas Forest Hills and Samba styles worn on football terraces linked sport to street identity.

PUMA

Puma was founded in the late 1940s by Rudolf Dassler following his split from his brother, Adi, who would go on to build Adidas (see page 114). While both brands came from the same beginnings, Puma developed a different character. Where Adidas focused on scale and long-term systems, Puma leaned towards speed, independence and competitive edge. From early on, the brand positioned itself as quick to react, willing to experiment and closely tied to individual athletes. That approach shaped Puma's identity over time. Rather than building a fixed archive of reference points, the brand has often responded to specific moments, sports and cultural shifts as they happened. Puma's output reflects this flexibility, moving between performance, lifestyle and fashion-led work without settling into a single lane.

SIGNATURE MODELS

Puma's most recognizable sneakers are defined by simplicity. Models such as the Suede, Clyde and Roma were designed with balance and wearability in mind, allowing them to move easily between sport and everyday use. The Puma Suede, in particular, became

RIGHT: Puma styles easily made the transition from their basketball origins to popular everyday wear.

PUMA
Limited Edition.
AVAILABLE AT JD SPORTS • ATHLEISURE • FOOTHOLD • GIRO'S
OFFICE • COBRA SPORTS • HARRODS • TOP TRAINERS • SCHUH
SO DON'T WEAR THEM OUT.

PUMA
KING PELE

PUMA

closely associated with breakdancing and early hip hop culture, valued for its grip, durability and clean shape. These shoes gained cultural meaning through use, shaped by the communities that adopted them.

INNOVATION STORIES

Innovation at Puma has tended to arrive in focused moments rather than long-running platforms. The brand has explored lightweight construction, low-profile designs and athlete-led development, particularly in football and athletics. In more recent years, collaboration has become an important tool, with designers and creatives helping to reframe familiar silhouettes without fundamentally altering their structure.

IDENTITY AND ADAPTABILITY

Puma's strength lies in its ability to shift emphasis while remaining recognizable. It has moved between elite sport, street culture and fashion with relative ease, adjusting its tone to suit different contexts. That adaptability has allowed the brand to stay visible across changing landscapes, defined less by permanence than by movement.

TOP LEFT: The Puma King football boot, associated with Pelé, was designed for control and durability.
BOTTOM LEFT: Puma Suede sneakers, widely adopted beyond sport into casual wear.

NEW BALANCE

New Balance has built its reputation quietly. Founded in Boston in the early twentieth century, the company focused on fit, function and comfort. From early arch supports to performance running shoes, its priorities were shaped by biomechanics and wearability, with an emphasis on getting the fundamentals right. While other brands expanded through marketing and athlete-led storytelling, New Balance developed credibility through consistency, earning trust among runners who valued reliability over image.

That approach has given the brand a distinct position within the sneaker landscape. New Balance has rarely tried to define trends. Instead, it has allowed performance needs, manufacturing standards and long-term use to guide its decisions, resulting in products that feel considered.

SIGNATURE MODELS

Many of New Balance's most recognizable sneakers sit within its running catalogue. Models from the 99X series, alongside silhouettes such as the 574, reflect a balance between support, cushioning and stability.

TOP RIGHT: New Balance chairman Jim Davis at the company's factory in 1995.
BOTTOM RIGHT: The New Balance 574, a core model balancing performance and lifestyle appeal.

ABOVE: Running shoes designed for durability and comfort underpin the New Balance range.

These shoes were designed to handle mileage, but their muted palettes and layered construction helped them transition naturally into everyday wear. Rather than being adopted through hype, they found an audience through comfort and familiarity, particularly among people who wore them daily.

INNOVATION STORIES

Innovation at New Balance tends to be incremental. The brand has refined cushioning systems, sole units and upper construction over time, favouring adjustment over overhaul. Its continued commitment to domestic manufacturing through New Balance Made has reinforced this mindset, placing value on process, materials and skilled labour. Advances are introduced to improve fit and performance.

CREDIBILITY AND CONTINUITY

New Balance occupies a space defined by trust. It is worn by athletes, workers and casual wearers alike, often for the same reasons. The brand's influence comes from use instead of visibility, shaped by people who return to its shoes for consistent performance. In a category driven by attention, New Balance stands out by prioritizing substance, allowing its reputation to grow through repetition rather than assertion.

VANS

Vans emerged from a simple idea: make shoes that people could buy, wear and rely on immediately. Founded in California in the mid-1960s, the brand began by producing footwear on site and selling it directly to customers, often on the same day. That closeness to everyday use shaped Vans from the outset, grounding the company in practicality and direct feedback from wearers.

As skateboarding grew through the 1970s, Vans footwear was adopted naturally by skaters who valued grip, durability and board feel. The brand responded to how its shoes were being used, allowing wear to inform design decisions over time. This exchange between product and practice became central to Vans' identity.

SIGNATURE MODELS

Vans' most recognizable shoes are defined by consistency. Models such as the Authentic, Era and Old Skool share flat soles, sturdy canvas or suede uppers and straightforward construction. Their forms changed little as they moved from skate parks into

TOP: Skateboarding champion Stacy Peralta in Vans in 1978.
BOTTOM LEFT: Vans Breakers were designed for breakdancing.
BOTTOM RIGHT: Vans Authentic with checkerboard pattern.

BREAKING OUT
Man, I need VANS
Breakers
Only For The Elite!
STYLE 439
STYLE 436
QUANTITY
STYLE NO.
SIZE
WIDTH
PRICE
TOTAL $
P.O. Box 729
Anaheim, CA 92805
Attn: JUNE TAPP
NAME
ADDRESS
CITY
STATE
ZIP
TELEPHONE #

ANS

wider circulation. Colour, pattern and wear became the points of variation, shaped by the individual rather than dictated by the brand.

INNOVATION STORIES

Innovation at Vans has been incremental and practical. Improvements to rubber compounds, padding and reinforcement were introduced to support skating while preserving familiar silhouettes. More recent performance models expanded the range, but the core designs remained visually stable and widely recognizable.

ROOTED IN COMMUNITY

Vans has remained visible by staying connected to the spaces where its shoes are worn. Skate parks, music venues and local scenes have played an active role in shaping how the brand is perceived. Rather than directing culture, Vans has grown alongside it, maintaining relevance through shared use and everyday presence.

LEFT: Vans Old Skool worn at a skate park, linking design directly to function and subculture identity.

CONVERSE

Converse began as a sportswear company long before sneakers carried cultural meaning. Founded in the early twentieth century, the brand established itself through basketball, producing shoes that were simple, durable and widely available. Its early success came from reach and familiarity, supplying a growing sport with a reliable standard that could be worn by anyone.

As athletic footwear developed and performance expectations increased, Converse's role shifted. Technical leadership moved elsewhere, but the brand's shoes remained in circulation, gradually separating from organized sport and entering everyday life. This transition unfolded through habit and repetition. Converse became familiar, then habitual, worn by people drawn to ease, affordability and a recognizable form.

SIGNATURE MODELS

The Chuck Taylor All Star defines Converse more than any other shoe. Its canvas upper, rubber sole and minimal construction have changed little, allowing it

RIGHT: The Converse Chuck Taylor All Star – in its original context on the basketball court (top and bottom right in 1950) – is one of the sport's earliest mass-adopted sneakers.

CONVERSE
Chuck Taylor
ALL STAR

to move easily across settings. Basketball courts gave way to music venues, art schools and city streets, with the shoe's simplicity making it adaptable to different identities and subcultures.

INNOVATION STORIES

Innovation at Converse has been limited and deliberate. The brand has focused on refining materials, improving comfort and exploring collaboration, while leaving core silhouettes intact. Updates tend to support wearability and relevance without altering the underlying shape.

CULTURAL ADOPTION

Converse occupies a distinctive position within sneaker culture. Its most recognizable shoes are no longer defined by their original purpose, but by how completely they have been absorbed into daily life. Worn across generations and contexts, Converse functions as a shared reference point, shaped by the people who continue to wear it in their own way.

LEFT: Converse sneakers worn in an infinite variety of settings demonstrate continued cultural relevance.

EXPANDING FIELD

For much of sneaker history, influence flowed from a small group of dominant sportswear brands. Performance credibility, athlete endorsement and scale shaped what people wore. That centre still exists, but the field around it has widened. Today, different brands have found space by focusing on specific needs instead of universal appeal.

BEYOND PERFORMANCE

One route has been through comfort-led performance. Brands such as HOKA and On have attracted runners and everyday wearers alike by prioritizing cushioning, stability and ease. Their shoes are engineered for movement, but their clean design and emphasis on comfort have helped them move beyond training alone. Performance no longer needs to look aggressive to be taken seriously.

Another shift has come from outdoor and technical footwear entering daily rotation. Salomon, long associated with trail running and hiking, has

TOP RIGHT: Salomon performance footwear influences contemporary streetwear through technical design.
BOTTOM RIGHT: Modern running silhouettes prioritize cushioning, stability and outdoor performance.

HOKA

found a wider audience as functional design has crossed into urban wear. Practical features, durable materials and utilitarian shapes have become part of everyday style, driven as much by lifestyle as by terrain.

Established performance brands have also been reinterpreted. ASICS has seen renewed interest in its running archive, with silhouettes valued for proportion, comfort and authenticity rather than novelty. Familiar models now sit comfortably alongside contemporary wardrobes, helped by a broader appreciation for technical heritage.

SHIFTING VALUES

Alongside performance, values have become a differentiator. VEJA represents a different approach altogether, where materials, sourcing and transparency define the product as much as design. The appeal lies not in technical claims, but in offering a clear alternative to conventional production.

Together, these brands illustrate how sneaker culture has opened up. There is no single path to relevance. Comfort, function, heritage and ethics now sit side by side, expanding the field and reshaping what people expect from the shoes they wear.

LEFT: Veja trainers are made using sustainable materials and transparent production practices.

Abloh, Virgil 84–7
Adidas 7, 15, 17, 26, 88–91, 114–19, 120
  Boost 89, 90, 117
  Forest Hills 119
  Gazelle 18, 19, 74–5, 74, 114
  Hu 118
  Kanye West collaboration 88-91
  Samba 18, 19, 114, 118
  Spezial 18
  Stan Smith 34–7, 114
  Superstar 14, 42–5, 114, 118
  Yamamoto collaboration 104–5
  Yeezy 88, 91, 118
    Boost 350 89, 90
    Boost 700 90
Air Force 1 54–7, 84, 92, 94, 96, 100–1, 108
Air Jordan 16, 26, 108, 112
  1 17, 52–3, 83, 84, 87, 96, 98, 102
  3 58–61, 81
  XI 82
Air Mag 83
Air Max 20, 96, 100
  1 72–3, 80
Air Presto 84
Air Trainer 1 82
Air VaporMax 85
Air Yeezy 88
All Star 30–3, 30, 33, 94, 132, 135
ASICS 139
  GEL-Lyte III 76–7
Authentic 128

basketball 6, 10, 13, 16–18, 24, 26, 52, 55, 56, 59, 60, 64, 67
  Adidas 43, 114
  Converse 31–2, 132, 133, 135
  Nike 17, 52, 55–6, 60, 64, 83, 108, 110, 113
  Puma 39, 120
Bowerman, Bill 47, 108

collectors 24, 25, 27
Comme des Garçons 92–5,
Converse 10, 17, 132–5
  All Star 26, 30, 31
  Comme des Garçons collaboration 92–5
Chuck Taylor All Star 30–3, 94, 132, 133, 135
Cortez 46–9, 46, 49, 108

Dassler, Adi 114, 115
Dassler, Rudolf 114, 120
Dior 102–3
Dunk 64–7, 94, 97, 98, 100
Dunlop 10

Era 128

football 18, 39, 75, 113, 114, 115, 117–19, 123
  Puma King 122
Fragment Design 96–9
Frazier, Walt 'Clyde' 12, 13
FUBU 14
Fujiwara, Hiroshi 96–9

Gazelle 18, 74–5, 74, 114
GEL-Lyte III 76–7, 76

Hatfield, Tinker 59, 72, 80–3, 96
high fashion 21, 81, 102
hip hop 7, 14, 18, 24, 26, 39, 40, 43, 44, 56, 63, 118, 123
HOKA 136
HTM project 96
Hu 118

James, LeBron 112, 113
Jordan, Michael 16, 17, 52, 59–60, 83, 112

Karl Kani 14
Kawakubo, Rei 92–5
Kilgore, Bruce 55
Knight, Phil 108

McCartney, Stella 118
Mitsui, Shigeyuki 77
Moore, Peter 52

New Balance 51, 124–7
  99X 51, 124
  574 124–5
  990 50–1
Nike 26, 80–7, 108–13
  Abloh, Virgil 84-7
  Air Force 1 54–7, 54, 57, 84, 92, 94, 96, 100, 108
  Air Jordan 108, 112
  Air Jordan 1 17, 52–3, 53, 83, 84, 87, 96, 98, 102
  Air Jordan 3 58–61, 58, 61
  Air Jordan XI 82
  Air Mag 83
  Air Max 96, 100

Air Max 1 72–3, 73, 80
Air Presto 84
Air Trainer 1 82
Air VaporMax 85
Air Yeezy 88
Comme des Garcons collaboration 94, 95
Cortez 46–9, 108
Dior collaboration 102–3
Dunk 64–7, 94, 97, 98, 100
Fujiwara, Hiroshi 96-9
Hatfield, Tinker 80-83
HTM project 96
Supreme collaboration 100–1
'The Ten' project 84, 86, 87
West, Kanye 88

Old Skool 62–3, 62, 128
On 136
Onitsuka Tiger Corsair 47

Parker, Mark 96
Puma 114, 120–3
Clyde 12, 120
King 122
Roma 120
Suede 14, 38–41, 120, 123

Reebok, Classic 68–71
Roma 120
Ronaldo, Cristiano 112, 113
Run-DMC 14, 44, 118, 119
running 6, 26, 47, 51, 68, 77, 108, 111, 117, 124, 126, 136, 137, 139

Salomon 136, 137, 139
Samba 18, 114
Simons, Raf 118
Smith, Mark 88
Smith, Steven 91
social media 18, 24, 27
Spezial 18
Stüssy 14
Suede 14, 38–41, 38, 41, 120, 123
Superstar 14, 42–5, 42, 45, 114, 118
Supreme 100–1

Taylor, Chuck 13, 31
tennis 6, 10, 35, 113, 114
'The Ten' project 84, 86
timeline 26–7

US Rubber (Keds) 10, 11

Van Doren, Paul 63
Vans 14, 128–31
Authentic 128, 129
Breakers 129
Era 128
Old Skool 62–3, 128, 130
Veja 138, 139

West, Kanye 88–91, 118
Williams, Pharrell 118
Williams, Serena 112, 113

Y-3 label 78, 104–5, 118
Yamamoto, Yohji 104–5, 118
Yeezy 88, 91, 118
Boost 350 89, 90
Boost 700 90

PICTURE CREDITS

The publishers would like to thank the following for permission to reproduce copyright material. All reasonable efforts have been made to trace copyright holders and to obtain their permission for the use of copyright material. The publishers apologize for any errors or omissions and will gratefully incorporate any corrections in future reprints if notified.

t: top, b: bottom, l: left, r: right

Alamy: 11, 126 adsR; 12, 121, 129bl Retro Ad Archives; 78 Associated Press / Zacharie Scheurer; 101 Wirestock, Inc; 109t Science History Images; 109b Associated Press.

Getty Images: 7 Janette Beckman; 8, 133t Bettmann; 15 Ron Galella; 16 Focus on Sport; 20 Hannah Peters; 49, 95t, 97, 137t Edward Berthelot; 50t chang; 81 20fifteen; 82t Dave Pedley; 82b Corbis/Chris Ryan; 87bl WWD/Penske Media; 87br Melodie Jeng; 95b Peter White; 103 Jay L Clendenin; 105 Arun Nevader; 113tl Adam Pretty; 113tr Copyright © 2024 NBAE (Photo by Jeff Haynes/NBAE via Getty Images); 113b Jonathan Moscrop; 115 t and bl ullstein bild; 115br William Vanderson/ Fox Photos/Hulton Archive; 116 Gotham/ GC Images; 119t Oliver Morris; 125t Boston Globe/Tom Landers; 129t Peter Cade/Central Press/Hulton Archive; 133br Curt Gunther/Archive Photos/Keystone; 137 Lucas Zarebinski/Footwear News/ Penske Medi.

Pexels: 28 shyam mishra; 33 Archaic Ki D; 37 HamZa NOUASRIA; 41 VVS ™; 53 Lee chinyama; 54t Cristiano De Luca; 66 Jonathon Burton; 74t, 89 Terrance Barksdale; 90t Erik Mclean; 98b Ox Street; 133bl Matheus Bertelli; 134 behrouz sasani.

Shutterstock: Front cover and 2, 69t xMarshall; 23 Stock by Fura26; 30t Adilson Sochodolak; 30bl kocetoiliev; 34t and b, 46b, 74b, 122b 2p2play; 42t seeshooteatrepeat; 42b artyaroslave; 46t Rama Rafael; 58t, 65t and b Node Hingprakhon; 58b phil_berry; 62t and b Nor Gal; 69b Only_NewPhoto; 73 ItzaVU; 85 Alina Boldina; 90b Moma okgo; 119b Red Union/Kobal; 125b Resul Muslu.

Unsplash: 19tl Giulia Perera; 19tr Marcus Kern; 19b SJ; 25t Warren Jones; 30br Gustavo Xavier; 38t and b, 110 Maria Fernanda Pissioli; 45 Alina Grubnyak; 50b Raul De Los Santos; 54bl and br Peter Albanese; 57 Sven Ciupka; 61 Sysoda Chau; 70 LexScope; 87t Karsten Winegeart; 93 Mnz; 98t SOLESTAGE CHECK; 106 BBiDDac; 129br Carmen Fu; 130 Doug Bagg; 138 Baptiste Buisson.

Also: 76 t and b: images supplied by ASICS, with thanks.
122: image supplied by Puma, with thanks.

AUTHOR ACKNOWLEDGEMENTS

This book draws on the work of designers, athletes and communities who have shaped sneaker culture over time. Thanks to the photographers, archives and image agencies whose work captures that history, and to the museums and institutions preserving it. Appreciation also goes to the editors and production team for their support throughout.

OTHER BOOKS AVAILABLE

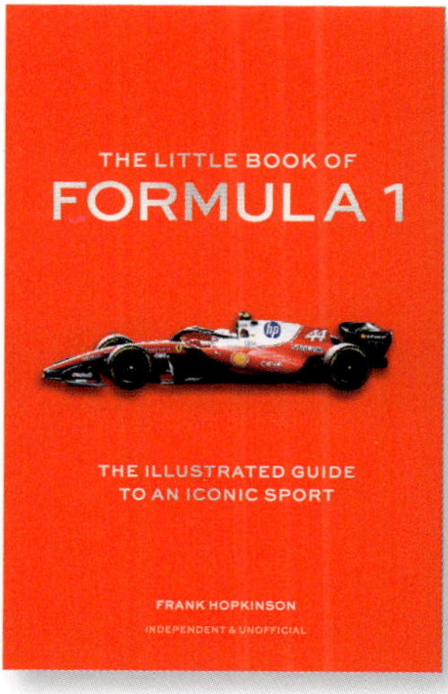

ISBN: 978-1-78840-699-4

ISBN: 978-1-78840-698-7

RAISING READERS
Books Build Bright Futures

Dear Reader,

We'd love your attention for one more page to tell you about the crisis in children's reading, and what we can all do.

Studies have shown that reading for fun is the **single biggest predictor of a child's future life chances** – more than family circumstance, parents' educational background or income. It improves academic results, mental health, wealth, communication skills, ambition and happiness.[1]

The number of children reading for fun is in rapid decline. Young people have a lot of competition for their time. In 2024, 1 in 10 children and young people in the UK aged 5 to 18 did not own a single book at home.[2]

Hachette works extensively with schools, libraries and literacy charities, but here are some ways we can all raise more readers:

- Reading to children for just 10 minutes a day makes a difference
- Don't give up if children aren't regular readers – there will be books for them!
- Visit bookshops and libraries to get recommendations
- Encourage them to listen to audiobooks
- Support school libraries
- Give books as gifts

There's a lot more information about how to encourage children to read on our website: **www.RaisingReaders.co.uk**

Thank you for reading.

hachette LIVRE

---

[1] OECD, '21st-Century Readers: Developing Literacy Skills in a Digital World', 2021, https://www.oecd.org/en/publications/21st-century-readers_a83d84cb-en.html

[2] National Literacy Trust, 'Book Ownership in 2024'. November 2024, https://literacytrust.org.uk/research-services/research-reports/book-ownership-in-2024